IMAGES OF ENGLAND

TRING
1951 – 2000

IMAGES OF ENGLAND

TRING
1951 – 2000

JILL FOWLER

Frontispiece: Without doubt one of the best-known Tring persons throughout the second half of the twentieth century was Nora Grace. When she died in August 2003 at the age of eighty-six she was referred to as 'Mrs Tring'.

A trained nurse, she married farmer Tom Grace in 1940 and Miswell Farm was often the site of garden parties and events in aid of charity. Nora was a tireless worker in the community. She started the Good Companions for the elderly and the Valiant Club for the disabled. She was a director of the Dacorum Council for Voluntary Services from 1984 and was perhaps best known as the Commandant of the Tring Red Cross. She joined the British Red Cross in 1945 and it was due to her enthusiasm and drive that the Red Cross Hall was built and opened in October 1971. The following year she was awarded the MBE in the New Years Honours List.

This photograph was taken, originally in colour, by Tring photographer Arthur Hyatt.

Dorian Williams, the last member of his family to live at Pendley Manor, was well known locally for several reasons. He was the master of the Whaddon Chase Hunt and his life-long knowledge of horses made him the ideal showjumping commentator, both in Britain and abroad. He introduced the first adult learning courses at Pendley and also started the annual Shakespeare Festival still enjoyed every year by thousands of visitors. This photograph shows Dorian in 1975 with artist Simon Ainstey and Simon's painting showing him with part of the manor in the background. In 1991, after Dorian had died, his widow, Jennifer, donated the painting to hang in the Pendley Manor Hotel where her husband had achieved so much in his lifetime.

First published in 2008 by
The History Press
97 St George's Place, Cheltenham,
Gloucestershire, GL50 3QB
www.thehistorypress.co.uk

Reprinted in 2008, 2019

© Jill Fowler, 2008

The right of Jill Fowler to be identified as the Author
of this work has been asserted in accordance with the
Copyrights, Designs and Patents Act 1988.

All rights reserved. No part of this book may be reprinted
or reproduced or utilised in any form or by any electronic,
mechanical or other means, now known or hereafter invented,
including photocopying and recording, or in any information
storage or retrieval system, without the permission in writing
from the Publishers.

British Library Cataloguing in Publication Data.
A catalogue record for this book is available from the British Library.

ISBN 978 0 7524 4620 2

Typesetting and origination by
The History Press
Printed and bound in England. by TJ International Ltd, Padsrow, Cornwall.

Contents

	Contents	5
one	1951–1960	9
two	1961–1970	33
three	1971–1980	61
four	1981–1990	89
five	1991–2000	109

Acknowledgements

Wendy Austin, Dennis Aldridge, Evelyn Barber, Mike Bass, John Bly, Pat and Eric Carlsson, Carol Cullen, Geoffrey Dicker, Joyce Dumpleton, Dick Fleckney, Mandy Giddings, Vera Goodall, Bob Grace, Nora Grace, Julie and Gilbert Grace, Stephen and Penny Hearn, Barbara Horton, Bob Hummer, Arthur Hyatt, Ada Jordan, David Kempster, Ron and Jackie Kitchener, Philip Lawrence, Cecelia Menday, Stirling Moss, Muriel Orton, Pitstone and Ivinghoe Museum Society, Doug Sinclair, Yvonne Spencer, Sylvia Rolfe, John Rotheroe, Derek and Janet Townsend, Ann Reed, Tring Rugby Club, *Tring Advertiser* and Tring Secondary Modern School. Special thanks to the *Bucks Herald*, Aylesbury and *The Gazette*, Hemel Hempstead.

The corner of Frogmore Street and Parsonage Place in the centre of Tring, photographed in 1982. At the time the restaurant was known as Foxy's Corner House. Now, still a restaurant, it has been renamed Tringfellows. Ten years before this picture was taken the business on the corner was Henry Johnson and Son, fishmongers. Henry moved here from his shop at No. 22 High Street in the late 1890s and when he retired, the business was carried on by his son-in-law William Keele until well into the second half of the twentieth century.

Introduction

When I attempted to record the first part of the twentieth century in Tring I had to rely on research in old newspapers and documents and the memories of older Tring people. I thought that a record of the next fifty years would be easier as I came to live in Tring in the early 1950s and married into a local family. I soon found that a lot happened in the next fifty years. Housing estates were added covering a large area of open space around the comparatively small market town and bringing in a lot of new people, many from London. New clubs and societies were founded and the Tring Festival and Victorian Evening were popular annual events. There were sports clubs to cater for all ages and abilities, and clubs especially for the elderly and the disabled.

Thanks to the generosity of local people I have managed to illustrate most of the years in the second half of the twentieth century, hopefully reviving some interesting memories for those with affection for the town of Tring.

one

1951-1960

Whatever one's views are on hunting with hounds there is no doubt that the beautiful horses and their smart riders, some ladies riding side-saddle, make a spectacular sight. It was said that when the Old Berkeley (West) Hunt met in early February 1951 outside the Rose and Crown Hotel, Tring, about 600 people turned out to see them. Here they are just moving off towards Pendley for the first draw.

In the summer of 1951, Tring Park Colts Cricket Club won the Goddard Trophy by beating Walton Way Cricket Club from Aylesbury. George Goddard, a well-known Tring shopkeeper, had given the cup to encourage young cricketers. Here Mr Goddard is presenting the cup to Brian Goodson who took four wickets in the match. Just beyond Brian are his twin sisters. By them is Brian Webb and looking over his shoulder is Mrs Goodson.

On 9 June 1951, a special fête was held for the Drayton Manor School for blind children. Godfrey Wynn, the well-known writer and broadcaster, opened the event and was presented with a gift by two of the children. There were teas and sideshows and £130 was raised to send to the Royal London Society for Teaching and Training the Blind, who were running the school at Drayton Manor. A few years later they moved to a residential school at Seal in Kent.

This photograph shows some of the children playing in an inflatable pool on the lawn.

Drayton Manor, on the outskirts of Tring, was a private home after the School moved to Kent.

Pat Moss came to Tring with her family in 1950. She already had a reputation as a successful young showjumper being 'Leading Juvenile Jumper of the Year' at Harringay on her brilliant pony 'Brandy of White Cloud'. When she progressed to the adult jumping she was equally successful, especially with her horses 'Danny Boy' and 'Ricochet'. As a boy, her brother Stirling was also a frequent winner in equestrian events, sharing his sister's love of horses. Here they are together with one of their horses.

Stirling and Pat in the driveway of White Cloud Farm. Stirling was already becoming well known in the motor racing world. He went on to become, to many, the most famous racing driver of all time. Pat also soon proved that she was as competent behind the wheel of a car as she was on a horse.

Above: In September 1951 a driver from Tate and Lyle, London, parked his Bedford lorry by the Grand Union Canal and went into the British Road Service Buffer Depot at New Ground, near Tring. The lorry contained an 8-ton load of sugar that was to be stored at the depot. When the driver returned he found his lorry had run about 200yds down the quayside and it was partly submerged in the canal. It was hauled up later but not surprisingly most of the sugar had dissolved.

Right: When King George VI died in 1952 there was genuine sorrow in Tring as in other parts of Britain. As a good-looking shy young man he had been forced into the unenviable position of King by the abdication of his older brother Edward VIII in 1936. He was admired for the way he tackled the task especially in the war years of 1939-45. He was greatly helped by Queen Elizabeth, later the Queen Mother. The King would be seen locally visiting serviceman in nearby RAF Halton.

Tring held a ceremony on the church square to pronounce the accession of Queen Elizabeth II. The High Sheriff of Hertfordshire, Brigadier Sir William Ackland, read the Proclamation, which was heralded by his own trumpeters in ceremonial uniforms. *God Save the Queen* was played by the Halton Apprentices military band. The High Street was closed to traffic, enabling nearly 1,000 people to watch the ceremony.

This photograph, taken from the window of the Rose and Crown Hotel is reminiscent of the ones taken on 19 July 1919 to celebrate the signing of the treaty of Versailles to officially end the 1914-18 war.

These three girls receiving a rosette from the Queen at the Windsor Horse Show in 1952 are Alison, Mary Rose and Marigold Peddie of the Manor House, Little Tring. They grew up with horses as their father, Lt Col. James Peddie, used to enter classes for show ponies, with success at major shows, including Herts. County Show. Their mother used to judge show pony classes locally. In 1966 Mary Rose won the class for small hacks with her horse, 'Harden Pride', at the Richmond Royal Horse Show. The same year she married Adrian Cole, the son of Dr and Mrs Christopher Cole, at Tring Parish Church. Adrian and Mary Rose still live at the Manor House where there have been members of the Peddie family for well over half a century.

Above: The Queen's Coronation was planned for the following year and Tring Council made up a Coronation Committee chaired by Cllr R.G. Grace to arrange the town's celebrations. In July 1952 the Council were told that the young Queen would be passing through Tring to visit RAF Halton to present the colours and inspect the airmen. The children lined the streets and houses and shops were decorated to greet her. Taken by Don Reed, the photograph shows the Queen as her car was passing the Tring crossroads.

Right: On 30 August 1952 Tring-born Ron Kitchener married his pretty bride, Jacqueline Warren, at St Mary's Church, Northchurch. Ron's brother, Arthur, was best man. The Kitchener family was well known in Tring, Ron's parents being very involved in local events.

Ron's career, after serving as a sergeant in the Guards, was in the insurance business, his name still over the High Street premises, now the Tring branch of the Nationwide Building Society.

Ron and Jackie can often be seen in Tring, where they still live. Since his retirement Ron has more time to devote to his great interest – the gathering and recording of Tring's local history.

Above: The teaching of senior school children at Mortimer Hill had started as early as 1949 but there were only a few huts there and many children were still being taught at the old school in the High Street. In 1953 it was decided to replace the huts with a purpose-built Secondary Modern School on the Mortimer Hill site. The building was completed in about three years by a local firm, Donald Lockhart, and the senior school moved into the new school early in 1957. There were later additions to cope with the continuous rise in student numbers in Tring. This photograph was taken in 1988.

Left: The headmaster in the early days was Mr D. Stanley Thomas who joined Tring School in 1942 and retired in 1968. He was always known as Stan and was an extremely popular headmaster. Among his staff he had the support of his wife, Eirlys, who was also a teacher.

Above: Tring celebrated the Coronation of Queen Elizabeth II on 2 June 1953. Bob Hedges had spent most of the previous day creating this magnificent display of hydrangeas and other flowering plants. Here he is standing in front of his Miswell Lane shop with his wife Ruby and his mother Ada. The shop is still a busy general store and is now called The Old Stables. In a class for the best decorated shop this one was the winner.

Right: One of the winners in the class for decorated houses was John Tugby of 60 Miswell Lane. This was his third win as he had decorated his house for the 1935 Jubilee of George V and for the 1936 Coronation of King George VI, winning both times. This time he shared the first prize with Mr and Mrs Bull of Langdon Street.

As part of the celebrations many streets had a party for the children. The weather on the day was not ideal and several 'street' parties were held in local halls. One of the only parties held in the street was at Icknield Cottages, New Mill. It was also the smallest with eight children from eight houses. In Albert Street they also had a fancy dress competition and one of the winners was little Hilary Prouse, seen here in her in her costume as an Indian girl.

One of the youngest entrants was four-year-old Michael Greaves, travelling in his 'royal' carriage.

Some of the mothers of New Mill who organised a party for the children. Back row: Vera Goodall, Hilda Kempson, Mrs Bulley, Florence McAndrew, June Robinson, Nellie Hearn and Nellie Butler. The two children on the right are Derek Hearn and Annette Seabrook.

Young Children at the New Mill Party. Back row: Vivian Price, Alan Frazier, Ken Seabrook, Michael Kempson, Brian McAndrew, Margaret Simpson. Front row: Gerald Rodwell, the Pearsall sisters (?), Clive Goodall.

In June 1953 the Memorial Garden was officially opened by Mr S. Marshall of the British Legion. The garden, on the site of Lord Rothschild's water garden, was made to commemorate the Tring men who were lost in the Second World War. Over 200 people attended the ceremony, many of them from families that had lost relatives in the war. After the opening there was a dedication by Reverend Lowdell, vicar of Tring. A feature of the memorial garden is the tall Wellingtonia tree. A native of California, where it is known as the 'giant sequoia', it was introduced to Britain in 1853 and named after the Duke of Wellington who had just died.

August 1954 saw the death of a much-loved maternity nurse, Nurse Shore, at the age of sixty-four. It was reported that she had brought nearly 1,000 babies into the world. She also ran the Tring Infant Welfare Centre. This early photograph shows her in the centre of a large group of Tring mothers with their babies.

In January 1954 it was reported that a draft plan for Tring Council's new Goldfield site showing fifty council houses and two old peoples' bungalows had been approved. There had been some delay at first due to some people preferring alternative uses for the green fields, but work on the first ten houses started in the autumn. Goldfield Estate was built by local builders, Harrowell and Sons. Here work is in progress. Bungalows are yet to be built in the foreground.

The year 1954 was a very good one for the Hastoe Badminton Club. They were top of the South West Herts. League and the Herts. area leagues. Standing left to right: Desmond Whitely, Fred Smith, Tom Mothersole, Jim Attryde, Keith Mitchener, Doug Booth. Sitting left to right: Kathleen Mothersole, Renee Tarmer, Carol Cullen (née Prior), Margaret Booth (née Hearn).

Above: One of the greatest advantages to lovers of the countryside in Tring is its closeness to canals and reservoirs. This peaceful scene shows Tring Pumping Station in the background.

Left: In July 1955 Nature Conservancy declared Tring Reservoirs as a 'Nature Reserve'. It recorded that there were over 5,000 winter residents including black-headed and common gulls, along with ducks, grebes, warblers etc. Local bird lovers found the title misleading as the Rothschilds still had 'shooting season' rights at the reservoirs resulting in the death of hundreds of birds and distress to people walking there at the time. This photograph shows the reservoirs on a winter's afternoon.

A lady looking at birds with her binoculars while the children look at the wildlife in the water, 1924.

Mr Richard Filter on the BBC programme *Town and Country* said that on visits to Tring Reservoir he had seen 101 different kinds of birds, including twenty-one different kinds of water birds, waders, gulls, terns etc.

Left: Harold Grace, whose family had had an ironmongers business in Tring since the eighteenth century, had done well in motor sports but 1956 was a very successful year for him. Early in the year he won the Riley Motor Club's Winter Rally which started at Brands Hatch in Kent. He drove a 2.5 litre Riley, and the course of nearly 40 miles included nine tests. He came first out of sixty-two competitors.

Below: In May of the same year he came third in the Daily Express International Trophy Race, again driving a Riley. The race was won by Stirling Moss so to be placed in the event was an achievement.

That was not the first time Harold had raced with Stirling. In May 1953 he came second in a race at Silverstone. Here they are at the start of the race, Stirling in car No. 40 and Harold in car No. 34. There the team race was won by Riley.

Right: Harold's son Gilbert inherited his father's enthusiasm for cars and he helped to prepare the winning Riley in the workshops at Grace and Son. Gilbert also successfully competed in races, taking over Harold's 1.5 litre Riley when he finished racing in 1960. Here Gilbert is seen in another role, that of a hockey player. This is perhaps not surprising as when his parents first met in the 1920s Harold was captain of the Tring Hockey Club and his mother Marjorie was captain of the Aylesbury Hockey Team. Gilbert continued the family hockey tradition by being an outstanding member of the Tring Hockey Club and he is still playing. He too played for the first team and was chairman of the club for eight years.

Below: Graces' ironmongery shop as it will be remembered by several generations of Tring shoppers.

Left: The 1950s saw the arrival of several well-known American actors to make films with the timeless background of Tring Park. Errol Flynn came to star in the *Dark Avenger* which was released in 1955. He played Prince Edward of Wales and most of the rest of the cast were well-known British actors. The film was described as 'a dashing costume piece' and most days horses could be seen galloping about the park.

Below: When Mr Alfred Moss and his family moved into the Home Farm in Park Road they renamed it White Cloud Farm. Mr Moss specialised in Large White pigs and in 1956 he sold a £200 breeding boar called 'Whitecloud Marshal 242nd' to a breeder in Switzerland. It was flown from London to Zurich, the first time live pigs had been exported to Switzerland for five years.

A few years later in 1963 three pedigree boars were sold to a government breeding centre in Budapest in Hungary and the same year two Large White boars and six gilts were sent to Portugal to start a breeding programme.

This photograph was taken at White Cloud Farm by Ann Matthews of Tring Camera Club.

At a meeting in September 1958 Tring Town Council were concerned that the High Street was dangerous at the crossroads with Akeman Street and Frogmore Street. Several suggestions were put forward. They included the installation of traffic lights, the introduction of a special speed limit and making Akeman Street a one-way street. None of these ideas were implemented but white lines and 'halt' signs were added to the side roads and local drivers know they should come out of the side streets with care.

One safety measure that was put into practice was the narrowing of the High Street by about 2½ft on the police-station side for about 200yds. This enabled the halt line in Akeman Street to be advanced, level with the opposite corner, thus giving drivers a better view.

In September 1958 Edward Wright, the eldest son of Mr and Mrs E. Wright of Miswell Lane, married Marjorie Spencer, the eldest daughter of Mr and Mrs F. Spencer of Dundale Road. They were married at Akeman Street Baptist Church. Edward, always known as 'Ted' was a popular member of Tring's police force. He had also always been a horse lover and his four beautiful grey horses were a familiar sight for many years grazing in fields near the Tring bypass.

In 1958 Herbert and Elizabeth Burch celebrated their sixty-fifth wedding anniversary. They were married at Tring Parish Church on 7 October 1893.

Mr Burch was employed at Lord Rothschild's Home Farm for over forty-nine years, first as a herdsman and then for twenty-six years as head cowman. For many years he successfully showed his charges at the Tring Show and in 1938 he was awarded a prize for the longest service by any farm employee in the district. He retired in 1939 and they moved from the lodge in Park Road to No. 5 Louisa Cottages.

Mrs Burch was from an old Tring family, she was formerly Miss Elizabeth Welling. On the day of their anniversary Herbert and Elizabeth received a telegram from the Queen.

Here they are with their young family. At the back are the boys, William and Charles, and at the front the three girls, Florence, Dorothy and Kitty.

The four stars of the *The Devil's Disciple* in Tring Park: Janette Scott, Kirk Douglas, Burt Lancaster and Laurence Olivier.

The Devil's Disciple, an adaptation of George Bernard Shaw's play, was released in 1959 and saw three famous actors coming to Tring. They were Burt Lancaster, Laurence Olivier and Kirk Douglas. The leading actress was Britain's Janette Scott and the story was set in the time of the American Revolution. For this film a small village complete with a church and churchyard was built in Tring Park. Crowds of Tring people would walk across the park to watch the filming and hopefully get an autograph or take a photograph of the stars. Laurence Olivier played the British commandant General John Burgoyne.

Above: In May 1960 it was announced that kart-racing was to be staged at Long Marston and the Three Counties Kart Club was formed. Many of the karts were made locally by Keele Engineering Co. Keele Karts were described as the Rolls Royce of kart-racing and eight were ordered by King Hussein of Jordan. Later in the year a British team went to Barcelona to compete in an international kart race. The first eleven places were taken by British drivers out of a field of forty-three and the British team took the team award. Tring drivers were Norman Ward, his son Nobby and Roger Keele Jr.

By 1960 Pat Moss had taken up rally driving and that year she had a conspicuous success when, with her friend and co-driver Ann Wisdom, she won the 3,000-mile Liege-Rome-Liege rally in an Austin Healey sports car. They were the first women's team to win the event. The same year they had already won the women's race in the Monte Carlo Rally and went on to win it for three consecutive years. Here they are receiving a cup from Princess Grace of Monaco, with Prince Rainier just behind his wife.

Later, at a cocktail party in London, given by Innocenti of Milan, Pat and Ann were each presented with a Lambretta scooter in recognition of their achievements in the Monte Carlo Rally, where they drove an Austin A40.

Opposite below: Young Roger Keele was a consistent winner in go-kart racing; his machine is almost hidden behind all his cups and trophies.

Above and left: The year 1960 saw the death of George Putnam of 4 Park Road at the age of ninety-four. He had been a member of the Tring Fire Brigade for over fifty years and its chief officer for twenty-eight years. He joined Tring Fire Brigade when it was formed in 1889 and retired in 1940 when Tring Council presented him with a certificate in appreciation of dedicated service. Mr Putnam was born in Tring. During the early part of his life he was a sergeant in the 2nd Volunteer Battalion Bedfordshire Regiment, no doubt good training for leading Tring Fire Brigade. Here he is with his team of fireman, winners of a competition for hose drill. Back row from left to right: 'Jock' Sear, Eddie Roberts, Eddie Brackley, Peter Farr, Harry Bull. Front row from left to right: Sid Lovell, George Hinton.

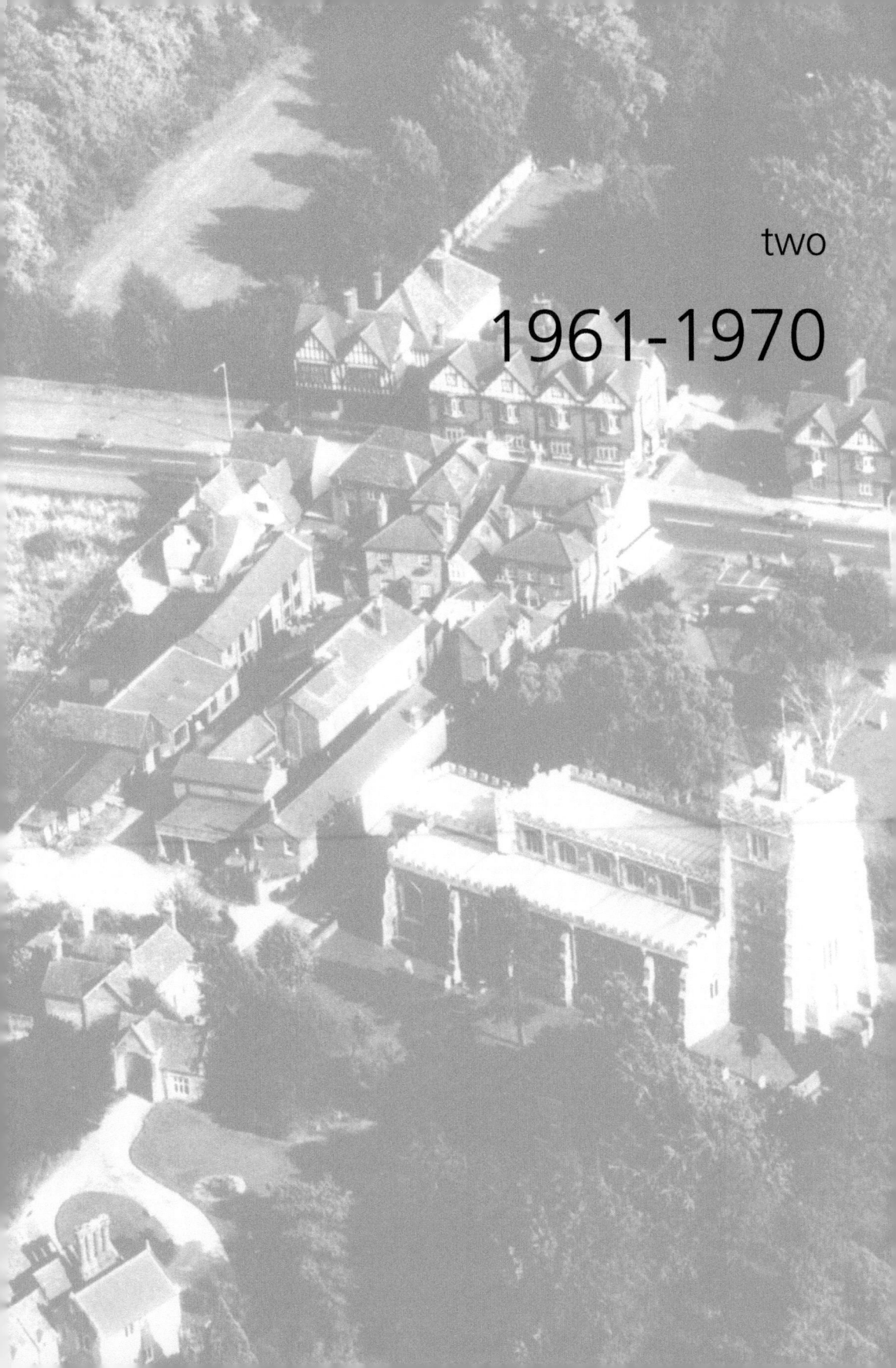

two

1961-1970

In the 1960s estates of modern houses were springing up and the town was expanding rapidly.

This view from the church tower shows roads of new houses including Friars Walk, Dunstan Hill and Deans Furlong, built on the site of Frogmore House, the home of the Butcher family, bankers of Tring. Butchers bank is now the NatWest in Tring High Street. An interesting old building in the front of this picture is the old bakery which has been preserved and adapted to make several comfortable homes.

It was often said that there was not much for young people to do in Tring. One thing that did interest the youngsters was the Tring Train Spotters Club. Here they are with train driver, Ken Poulton in May 1961 about to go on an outing.

They went to Kings Cross Station where they toured the sheds and looked at the latest diesel engines. The steam trains in those days were a more familiar sight at Tring Station.

The train spotters met several well-known people at the station including pop singer Cliff Richard and Arsenal footballer Alec Forbes. Here they are getting an autograph from guitarist Bert Weedon.

The winters in the early 1960s were severe with heavy snowfalls. It was reported that 1963 was the worst year since 1881. Then three express trains were buried in snow in Tring cutting and it was said that the frost was so hard that ducks were frozen to the ground.

The winter of 1963 was very hard with snow and ice lasting for some time. That year boys from Osmington School, then in Christchurch Road, built a 10ft-high igloo and slept in it.

In 1968 there was said to be the worst snowfall since 1963 and travelling conditions were chaotic. The Council was criticised for the state of Tring High Street but the heavy traffic had compacted the snow into solid ice, making it difficult to remove. Later large amounts of salt were purchased and stored for use when needed.

The children enjoyed the snow. They took their toboggans to Tring Park and some people even skied on the slopes.

Right and below: For those who did not have to travel the snow made the buildings in Tring look really picturesque. Here is the Castle public house and the Louisa Cottages, both in Park Road.

In 1962 Tring's fireman welcomed the opening of the purpose-built fire station in Brook Street. Before they had been stationed at the Market House in the centre of Tring but it was too small for the fire engine and lacked the facilities of the new building. The new station had a drying room for wet clothes, shower baths and a recreation room and kitchen. The builders were a local firm, F.W. Metcalfe.

The firemen are, from left to right: Jock Graffen, Ken Carlisle, Bill Giddings, Doug Sinclair, Paddy Foster, Charlie Cummings, Tom Saunders, Roy Robinson, Wally Rance, Dennis Bradding, Dudley Fulks, John Foskett, Bill Gosling.

Over the years the Fire Brigade gave demonstrations in schools and at events. Here they are at the Rose and Crown Hotel during Tring's first ever Festival in July 1973. The second vehicle from the left is Hertfordshire Fire Brigade's 1935 Leyand Fire Engine which had been on active service at St Albans from new and was retired in the late 1960s. Children were allowed to sit in the driving seats of the fire engines.

This happy couple are Don and Ann Reed after their wedding at Berkhamsted Registry Office on 29 May 1963. Don, a photographer, had his shop Reed Photography in Akeman Street. At least two generations of Tring people had their portraits, weddings and parties photographed by Don and his team. For several years he specialised in taking photographs at equestrian events all over the country.

This photograph of Princess Anne on her pony 'Bandit' was taken by one of Don's photographers at a pony club event in Berkshire in 1962. It was the first photograph of the princess jumping with her pony to be published in the national press.

Above and below: Pitstone Windmill is a landmark in the countryside as you drive from Tring to Ivinghoe. A post mill, it has the date 1627 on it and is said to be the oldest mill in the British Isles.

The year 1963 saw the formation of the Pitstone Restoration Fund to restore the mill which had been badly damaged in the violent storm in 1902. Belonging to the National Trust, to whom it was given in 1937, it stood on land belonging to Jeff Hawkins of Pitstone Green Farm. He and fellow enthusiasts raised the money for the repairs and did a lot of the work themselves. The sails, which were fitted in 1966, were made by carpentry students at Aylesbury College. They have a span of about 50ft and were made of Douglas fir and Baltic redwood.

There was still a lot of work to be done to get the windmill in working order and it was only in 1970 that it was ready. On 31 August that year they actually ground corn there, the first time for sixty-eight years. In September the fully restored windmill was officially opened by Lady Davidson, the Conservative MP for many years.

In October 1963 Parsonage Farm was pulled down to make way for Bishop Wood School. The farmhouse, seen here, was a historic building and in the eighteenth century was thought to be the Friary or lodging house for the visiting friars of Faversham. It was later the home of the curates of Tring. In the 1830s navvies working on the London to Birmingham railway were billeted there. From the 1860s there were numerous farmers here, more recently including Frank Grace and Arthur Lipscomb.

Bishop Wood School, soon after it was built.

Bishop Wood School was named after the Ven. C.T.T. Wood who became vicar of Tring for twelve years before he became Archdeacon of St Albans in 1942. He was made Suffragen Bishop of Bedford in 1948. Here is the school after it had been considerably enlarged.

In February 1963 Pat Moss, then described as 'Britain's top girl rally driver' came home to White Cloud Farm with her husband-to-be Erik Carlsson. They had announced their engagement during the Snow Rally being held in Finland. Erik, a friend of Stirling's, was also a very successful rally driver, having won the Monte Carlo Rally for two years in succession. They were married in the summer the same year. Here they are at home cleaning some of their trophies.

Photographer Don Reed after a trip to take aerial photographs over Tring. He was usually seen with a camera but here it was lent to his pilot, Jimmy Wilcox, to take this photograph. Jimmy was one of the youngest people in the country to get his pilot's licence. At the time the Wilcox family were running the Crows Nest restaurant at the top of Tring Hill. The Crows Nest, now a motel, is still a popular and busy restaurant.

One of the series of photographs taken by Don during the flight. The Louisa Cottages and the Museum can be seen at the front, the Mansion's old stable block to the right and the Parish Church in the distance.

Above and opposite, left and right: In Tring we are never far from a canal. Now used solely for pleasure they made ideal venues for filmmakers depicting early days on the waterways. The 1964 film *The Bargee* starred Harry H. Corbett as a canal barge casanova, Hemel Pike. He had previously gained fame as the son in *Steptoe and Son*. Some of the filming was done at the Toll House, Marsworth, the home of Evelyn Barber, well known in Tring when she had a grocery and florist's business. The first photograph shows the team filming in front of the house. In the second on the next page: Hugh Griffiths plays the fearsome Joe Turnbull whose daughter, Christine, played by Julia Foster, eventually wins the heart of the bargee. Other well-known stars in the film included Eric Sykes, Eric Barker, Miriam Karlin, Una Stubbs and Derek Nimmo. The third picture shows Evelyn with Harry H Corbett.

Opposite below: In the summer of 1964 it was announced that the Summer House in Tring Park was to be moved and the central part, with the portico, was to be re-erected in an open part of the park. It was said to have been built during the ownership of the Tring Park Estate by Sir William Gore. He succeeded Henry Guy, Groom of the Bedchamber to King Charles II, and laid out the ornamental design of the park.

The Hon. J. Rothschild gave permission for the summerhouse to be moved but in November the same year it was concluded that the considerable expense could not be justified. The remains of the building can still be seen in their original position by walkers going across the park up to Wigginton.

Above: On 5 November 1964 Hastoe Mill was gutted by fire and the building, said to be 100 years old, was destroyed. It took twenty men from Hemel Hempstead fire brigade seven hours to extinguish the fire completely, and about 300 tons of corn and animal feeding stuff was lost in the blaze. Police investigated the fire but the date may have suggested that a stray firework could have been the cause. The remains of the mill stood derelict for some time. The area has now been redeveloped but the mill was not used again.

Left: The first girl in the Berkhamsted and Tring District to become a Queen's Guide, in 1965, was sixteen-year-old Hillary Prouse of Windmill Way, Tring. She was a Brownie in the Tring Pack for three years and had been a Girl Guide for five years. Here she is at the Girl Guides' divisional church parade in 1964. There she was the leader of the Robin Patrol, 1st Tring Company and had already won her first class badge and all-round cords. To be a Queen's Guide she had to study hard to become proficient in many subjects.

Right and below: In September 1965 it was announced that the railway line to Tring was to be electrified in 1966 and when electrification was completed in 1967 the line would go from Euston to Manchester and Liverpool. Here the roadway at New Ground is being removed so that it can be raised before electrification of the railway beneath.

Above: Members of the Tring Train Spotters Club can be seen visiting the site and taking photographs.

Left: Bob Hedges by his greenhouses just before they were demolished to make way for the shopping parade. As well as running a busy shop Bob was actively involved in local affairs. He was an Independent Councillor for many years, with special interest in providing recreational facilities for local people, and young people in particular. He was president of Tring Corinthians Football Club, chairman of Tring Horse Association, involved in running Tring Youth Club and chairman of the local Boy Scouts Group. Another important role was that, as a member of the Tring Sports Development Committee, he worked hard to establish the sports centre at Pendley, now enjoyed by many local people. Beyond the greenhouses can be seen the backs of the shops in Western Road.

Above and below: In 1966 the new shopping parade was built at the bottom of Miswell Lane. It replaced Robert Hedges' greenhouse that extended from his shop, now The Old Stables, almost to Goldfield Road. This is the parade in 1969 when Robert Hedges had the first two shops, selling home and garden equipment. The ornamental cherry trees are now mature and provide a beautiful sight in the spring with masses of pink blossom.

This beautiful horse, 'Ansioso', was stabled at Pendley Manor in September 1966 when it was in quarantine, having come from Spain. Its rider, Senor Nuno Oliveira, the famous Spanish dressage rider, had come to give a display of advanced horsemanship at the Horse of the Year Show. He and his groom were staying at Pendley. Here Senor Oliveira and 'Ansioso' are performing for Tring photographer Mike Bass in the grounds of Pendley Manor and the picture later appeared in the *Bucks Herald* newspaper.

Opposie above: Early 1967 saw the destruction of Wigginton Manor on the corner of Brook Street and Mortimer Hill. It is shown here on the right before considerable improvements were made to turn it into the impressive house it was at the time it was demolished. Earlier, several small businesses had been carried on there and Wigginton's legal affairs dealt with, hence its name, although it was not a manor house nor in Wigginton. A local paper at the time showing the ruined building said that the work was being done to improve the Robin Hood crossroads.

Opposite below: The Market Garage expanded its premises to replace the house and a new road, Nursery Gardens was built behind it. The second photograph, taken in June 1971 gives almost the same viewpoint of Brook Street.

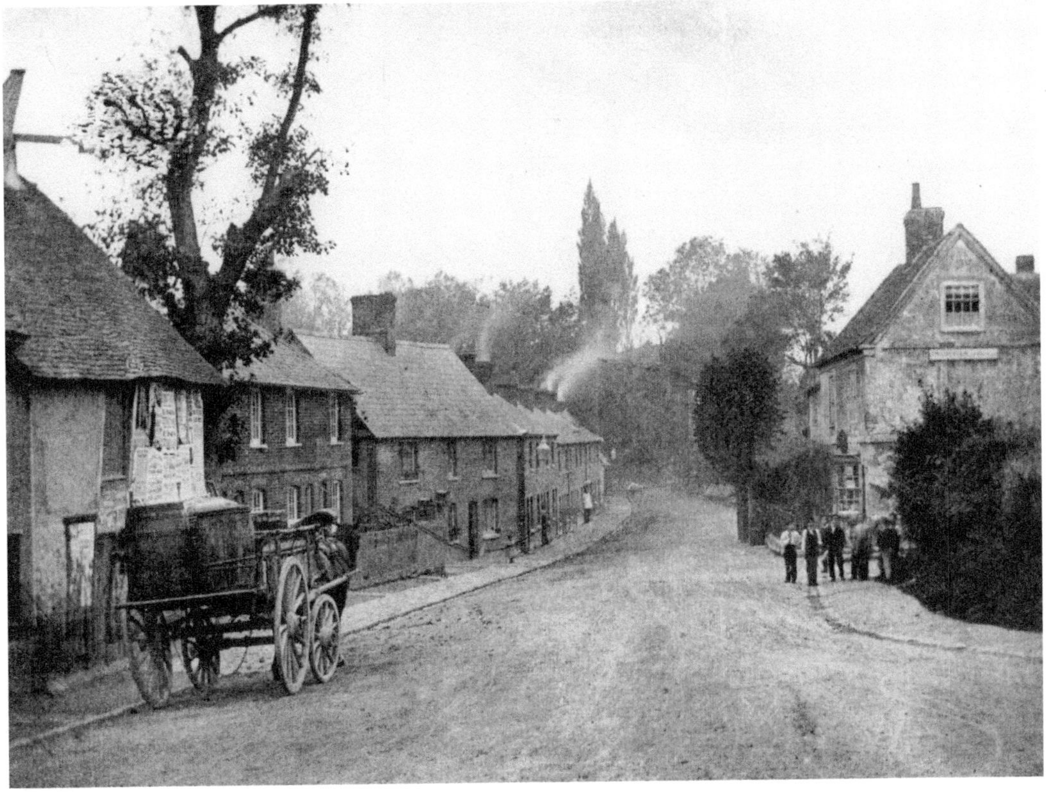

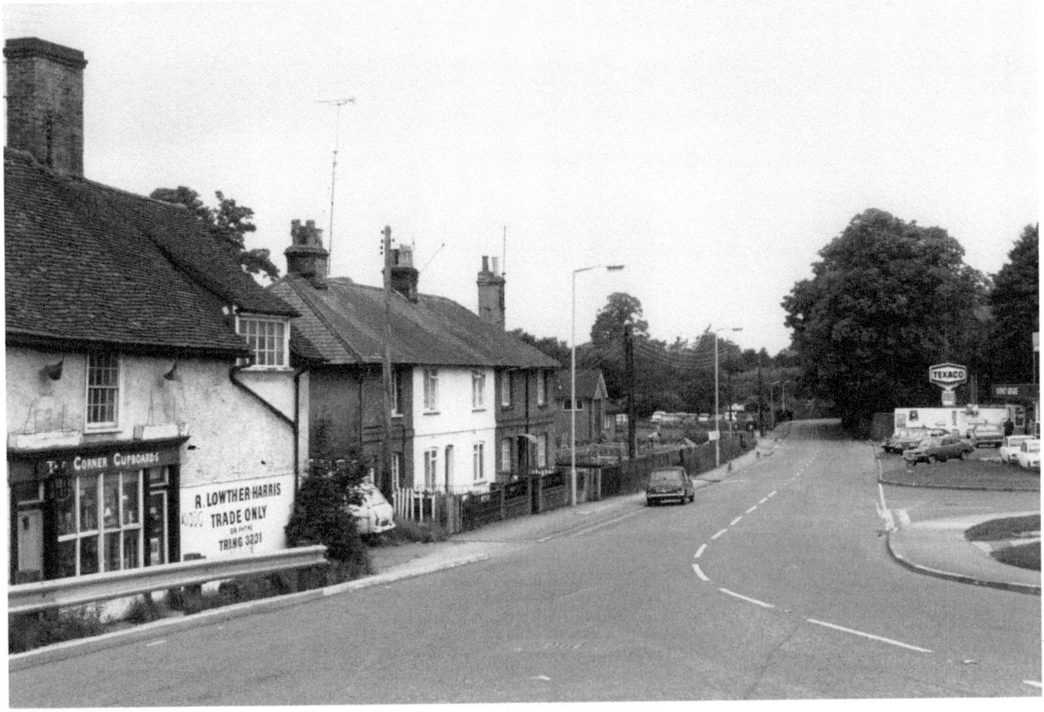
CORNER CUPBOARDS
R. LOWTHER-HARRIS
TRADE ONLY
TRING 3231
TEXACO

Frederick Hearn of Fox Road, Wigginton, was described by the local paper as 'probably the village's best known personality' when he died in August 1967. This came as no surprise, for he operated a milk round in Wigginton for thirty years. He was born in the village and lived there all his life.

One of his sons is Stephen Hearn who is now very well known in Tring for his business, Tring Market Auctions, in Brook Street, where interesting, useful and rare items are regularly sold.

Here milk is being delivered to The Greyhound, still a popular public house in Wigginton.

Right: The Bly family have been well known in Tring for several generations. John Bly married Virginia Fisher from Aylesbury on 15 September 1967. They are seen here at the gate of the Bell Inn, Aston Clinton, where the reception was held.

As well as running a long-established business in Tring High Street, John's grandfather, also named John, and John's father, Frank, also served on Tring Council for many years, and they were also Chairman of the Council for some time.

John is today well known as a furniture expert on TV programmes like *Heirloom* and *The Antiques Roadshow*, and Virginia, a keen gardener, opens their lovely garden to the public to raise money for charity.

Below: Tring Council had been asking for a pedestrian crossing for some time and the site by the Midland Bank was chosen by the Ministry. The Council was surprised that they were allowed two crossings; the other one was in Western Road. Tring now has four pedestrian crossings.

In 1968 fifteen-year-old Margaret Horton was a star in the tennis world. She won the ladies' singles in the Tring Lawn Tennis Clubs Championships and she went on to win the ladies' doubles with her mother, Barbara.

In August the same year Margaret won the Hertfordshire under-sixteen championship at Harpenden. The following year she was selected to play in the Hertfordshire under-eighteen team. The local paper described 1969 as 'a season overflowing with success'. That year she reached three finals at Tring and won them all; the ladies' singles, the ladies' doubles with her mother and the mixed doubles with Peter Mellor. She also won the Herts. County Junior singles championships, and as well as local success Margaret won the under-eighteen singles and girls' doubles at Plymouth.

In 1970 she became the Tring Club's ladies' champion for the third year running and she and her mother also held on to the Ladies Challenge cup.

Margaret and her mother at the tennis club about to be presented with the Ladies Challenge cup. In November 1971 Margaret married Chris Lawson and she and Barbara continued their success in Tring for a further five years. Later they played on grass courts at Halton.

Tring Lawn Tennis Club is still flourishing in the town, encouraging young players to become future champions, or, if they can't match Margaret Horton's achievements, enjoy an invigorating game of tennis.

Right: One of Tring's best-known cricketers was Fred Howlett. He joined Tring Park Cricket Club in 1919. He was a fast bowler and a hard hitter and captained the 2nd team before securing a place in the 1st team. He gained county honours by playing for the Herts. Juniors.

His best batting performance was 149 not out against a Hemel Hempstead team in the 1920s and in the 1930s he shared a stand of 176 with Albert Kempster in a match against Chipperfield. In 1960, when he was nearly sixty-one years of age, he gave up playing and became an umpire.

Below: In 1969 Tring Park Cricket Club held a dinner to celebrate Fred's fifty years with the club and he was photographed with a group of his colleagues, most well known in their day for their cricketing prowess.

Back row from left to right: Fred Plumeridge, Jimmy Rance, David Kempster, Lionel Hitchings, Derek Whitehead, Len Hinton. Front row from left to right: Pete Tyrell, Stan Scales, Fred Howlett, Doug Westcott, Bill Green.

Above and below: In May 1969 an application was made to the council to demolish the old vicarage and build a modern house and garage. This caused considerable consternation. Many people wanted to save the old building, though some thought it 'an over-expensive white elephant'. Two years later there was another application to include a new church hall, the conversion of the existing vicarage into offices and building a new wing of offices. It would ensure the preservation of the vicarage. The new hall to be built on the old garden was to be shared by the Anglicans and Methodists in Tring, and the offices were to become the headquarters of the Sutton Housing Trust. The area still retains much of its old-fashioned charm with the pond and fountains in the courtyard.

This view of the church from the air shows the vicarage and the gateway in the bottom left corner before any work was started.

Silk Mill Farm in 1938. In September 1968 a plan to develop Silk Mill Farm was submitted to Tring Council Planning Committee. The applicants wanted to build 353 houses at a density of twelve per acre. In November 1970 the Greater London Council bought 40 acres of Silk Mill land and announced they would build a housing estate for about 2,000 Londoners, known as its 'overspill' population. Some of the people of Tring were horrified at the prospect, suggesting that 'with these people will come vandalism, bingo, drunkenness and other sordid goings-on'. Others said that they should be given a chance, whoever came to Tring.

The dispute rumbled on and in the following year the GLC made concessions in the density of the housing. When the estate was built and the Londoners moved in they soon fitted in with the local community.

In 1968 a fund was started by parents and friends of pupils at Bishop Wood School to build a training pool for children. The money was raised with the help of local organisations like the Eight of Herts. and the official opening was performed by Cllr Philip Fells and his wife in 1970 and the pool was 'christened' by throwing Colin Kendrick, Chairman of the Parents Committee, into the water. Then the crowd threw coins into the pool and a team of children dived in to retrieve them.

Later an indoor swimming pool was built at Mortimer Hill School, but many of Bishop Wood's young pupils learned to swim in this outdoor pool.

The school swimming pool fund-raising fête in mid-June 1970 was opened by Harry H. Corbett. Here he is joining in one of the sideshow games. The fête was organised by the Eight of Herts. A donation to raise funds was a stage engagement ring given by actress June Whitfield and worn in the series *The Best Things in Life*.

This photograph of members of the Tring Red Cross Detachment was taken in March 1970 as part of an exhibition at the Kings Hall, Berkhamsted, to mark the centenary of the Red Cross Society on 11 April. A week before, thirty-five members from Tring had been presented with first aid certificates by the Medical Officer Dr D. Thallon, seen here sitting next to the Commandant, Nora Grace.

Back row from left to right: Jo Ridley, Mrs Yates, Dena Reeves, Molly Percival, Rosemary Duck, Jean Kitchener, Joan Allen, Erica Guy.

Third row from left to right: -?-, -?-, Beryl Perkins, Mary Watson, Mary Chapman, Ruby Boniface, Gladys Hull, Margo Baines, Shirley Blake, Rosemary Culbert, -?-, -?-.

Second row from left to right: Janet Ford, Joan Cole, Joan Watts, Vera Hare, Nora Grace, Dr Thallon, -?-, Betty Wood, Mrs Whittaker.

Front row from left to right: -?-, Mrs Hermon, Joan Betts, Peggy Morris, -?-, Janet Grace, -?-, -?-.

Above and below: There had been a railway station at Long Marston but by 1970 the booking office and waiting room had been disused for some time, since the railway closed down. That year an application was made to convert the old Marston Gate station premises into living accommodation, but it was turned down. The surveyor said it was a dilapidated building and the only thing feasable was to pull it down.

three

1971-1980

The two closed shops in June 1971 that were to be demolished to make way for the entrance to the new shopping centre, Dolphin Square. They were Clements, jewellers and clock and watchmakers since 1773; and Sanders, the fruiterers and greengrocers, previously Gilbert Graces Ironmongers shop in the nineteenth century.

A view of the back of these shops, on the right, as they were being demolished. In the centre is the entrance to the yard behind the Bell Hotel. The banks opposite are still there, now the NatWest and the HSBC.

A close view of the buildings being cleared to make way for the entrance to Dolphin Square.

Work has started on Tring's new town centre. Frogmore Street can be seen in the background.

Tring had held its Friday market in the High Street for very many years. Here the stalls are against the mansion wall. There would have been stalls on the opposite pavement as well. When the new car park in the Lower High Street was built on what was known as the Green Man meadow, the market moved there. The first Friday that the traders set up their stalls on the car park was 30 April 1971.

When the Tring bypass was finally opened in 1975 the headline in the local paper said 'After 40 years – Tring's by-pass'. It had certainly been discussed for many years and had aroused strong feelings. Many people had objected to the southern route that would cut across Tring Park, thus to many people spoiling it. The northern route was equally unpopular, cutting through villages and disturbing the peace of Tring reservoirs. This photograph of Tring crossroads, taken in June 1971, shows why local people were demanding a bypass. It was finally started over two years later.

In October 1971 the new Red Cross building in Pond Close was opened. It was on land given by Mrs Philip Fells and the building appeal to raise £20,000 had been launched only a year before. Nora Grace, seen here, felt that there was a need for a new meeting place for the Good Companions Club for the over seventies and the Tring Red Cross, both of which she keenly supported. The Red Cross Hall is still used regularly by many Tring clubs and societies.

The building was designed by architect Mr E.T. Dowling, whose wife was the Red Cross Divisional Director. The chairman of the building appeal fund was Philip Fells. The official opening ceremony was performed by Major-General Sir George Burns, Lord Lieutenant of Hertfordshire, seen here talking to some of the nurses.

Opposite and above: Early in 1968 it was announced that an extension to the museum was proposed. The council welcomed the idea of enlarging the museum but felt that the design was not in keeping with the general architecture of the old building. Cllr McAndrew felt that it looked like a multi-storey car park.

Work started on the £400,000 project in January 1970. Local objections about the design were overruled by the Ministry of Works. The old north wing of the museum was pulled down in March. It was hoped that the new building would be ready by the end of 1971 and the valuable bird collections from the British Museum would have a new home at Tring by mid-1972.

In July 1972 the Duke of Edinburgh came to Tring to open the new ornithological section of the museum. Here he is accompanied by Sir George Burns, the Lord Lieutenant of Hertford. The line-up to greet the Duke included Cllr Edward Binks, Chairman of Tring Council, and his wife, Mr James Allason, MP for Hertford, Mr K.W. Tavener, Clerk to the Council, and Mr C.L. Rance, former caretaker of the museum.

Above and left: In 1972 the gatehouse to the old vicarage had got into a very poor state and it was considered to be dangerous. It had been built in the early nineteenth century by the Reverend Charles Lacy, then vicar of Tring. When it was suggested that it should be demolished there was an outcry, people protesting that it was a focal point near the church.

Right: The gatehouse was rapidly crumbling away and it was decided to demolish it and then to reinstate it. The building work was done so well that many people did not realise that the old gatehouse had been replaced, though these photographs taken at the time show the demolition in progress.

Below: The gatehouse still makes an impressive entrance to Sutton Court and the Anglican Methodist Hall.

Tring Rugby Club was formed in 1964 and their first match was against the Bacavians. The team in those days included Ken Laidler, who later became their coach, and Dr D. Thallon, in the centre here, a popular doctor in Tring. Tring won by thirty-six points to nil. A little later they beat Oxford Old Citizens, at Oxford, 3-0. There Dr Thallon was the only scorer and soon he was chosen to play for Hertfordshire, having been a regular player for Surrey County.

Over the years the Rugby Club had more successes and the odd loss. At the end of 1971-72 season Mike Blake, pictured here, was presented with the annual Chairman's Trophy for the outstanding player of the year. This photograph shows the team for the 1972-73 season with some of the team's officials. An outstanding win, one of many that season, was their defeat of Milton Keynes in March, 32-0.

Back row (standing) from left to right: Mike Hulme (Sec), Ifor Dando, Chris Wallis, Phil Plant, Peter Ogie, John Rush, Bernard Axford, Mike Blake, Peter Springett, Richard Podd, Tony Burch, Ken Laidler (coach), Peter Hutton (Chairman).

Front row from left to right: Angus Findlay, Tony Branwhite, John Kelly, Frank Campbell (Capt.) John Ramsbottom, Eric Craigie, Mike Plant.

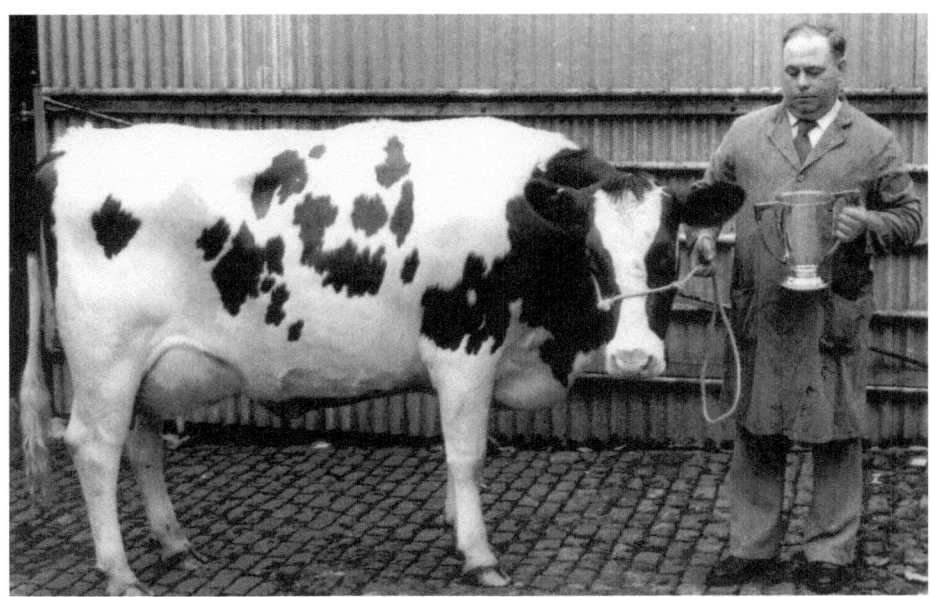

For the third time in the past four years up to 1972 Mr and Mrs Norman Rolfe, Icknield Farm, Tring, won the first prize for the best-kept farm under 200 acres. The annual competition was organised by the Chiltern Hills Agricultural Association and the Chiltern Cup was presented to the winner. Icknield Farm had 130 acres and a herd of British Friesians, specialising in milk production.

Mr and Mrs Rolfe's daughter Sylvia was consistently successful in local horse shows, mainly with her two ponies 'Murphey' and 'Stardust'. It would not be possible to list all her successes, particularly in the 1970s, but in a Tring Horse Show in June 1971 she came first in the class for the best rider under sixteen and in the family pony class, both times on Stardust. Here she is seen receiving the Presidents Cup for the family pony class, which she had won for three years in a row. It is being presented by Mr Julian Marshall. At the same show she was second in the working pony class, on Murphey. The next month Sylvia competed at Wigginton Horse Show and won six classes in the gymkhana classes for children thirteen years and under and three classes in the open events. Later in 1977 she won the small hack class at the Royal International Show at Wembley, on Creden Masterpiece.

Above and below: In the spring of 1973 work started on the reconstruction of the canal bridge near Tring Station. The original was built towards the end of the eighteenth century and it was widened about 100 years later. The reconstruction programme was due to be completed by October 1973 and as a temporary measure a Bailey bridge was put in place to take the traffic.

Above: At the end of March 1973 work started on the Pendley Sports Centre project after about six years of planning since the trustees of the Pendley Estate generously made 28 acres available for sporting purposes in Tring.

A sixty-five-year lease was signed and a peppercorn rent was agreed. Here Mrs Anne Adams, wife of Dr Michael Adams, lifts the first spadeful of soil on the Cow Lane site. Shown here are, from left to right: Dr Adams, John Holifield (representative of the Pendley Estates Trustees), Len Dean (chairman of Tring Bowling Club), Mrs Adams, Robert Hedges (chairman of the Centre trustees), Charlie Watkin (secretary of Tring Bowling Club), and Gordon McAndrew (centre trustee). The centre was officially opened on Saturday, 11 May 1974 by Dorian Williams.

Right: Ralph Seymour was well known in Tring. He was the manager of Mead's Flour Mills at New Mill, and chairman of the governors at Tring School. He was a member of Tring Urban District Council for several years, during which he served as chairman of the council. In April 1973 he was ordained deacon of the Tring Parish Church where he had been a reader for the previous thirty years. The ceremony of ordination was performed at the Church by the Bishop of Bedford, the Rt Reverend John Hare.

Mrs Cecilia Bly sitting in the yard at the back of the antique business she ran with her husband in Brook Street. The Corner Cupboard, next to the Robin Hood public house, is now the premises of the estate agents, David Doyle. Mrs Bly was born in Tring and had lived there until May 1972 when she went to live with her daughter in Anglesey. She died there less than a year later, aged eighty-four. Mr and Mrs Bly were well known in Tring. They bought and restored the Old Forge, High Street, Tring for their retirement. Mrs Bly's husband, Frederick, known as 'Bob' died in 1964 aged seventy-nine. She left two daughters and five grandchildren.

May of 1973 saw the tragic death of Robert George Wright, born in Tring and very well known in the town as he had been the senior partner in the garage Wright and Wright since 1920. He was killed in a road accident involving a lorry at the age of ninety-two, and had been on a visit to Blenheim Palace with two of his daughters. This early photograph shows the Wright family, completed by the baby Hilda. On the back row are Trevor, Muriel, Connie and Madge. In the centre is their mother Mary with George holding Hilda. At the front are Doris, John and Ruby. This photograph was taken on a plate camera in the early 1920s by Noel Orton, who later married Muriel.

Wright and Wright's garage in the 1960s before it changed hands at the beginning of 1969. The new owner specialised in the sale of Hyundai cars. For the first time since 1910, when George's cousin Albert went into partnership with George Parrott, who founded the firm in 1870, there were no members of the Wright family as directors.

By 2000 Wright & Wright's garage had closed and three blocks of Georgian-style semi-detached villas had been built. They were named 'Wrights Villas' to commemorate the garage they replaced, and prices started at £305,000. Some people criticised these houses as "modern copies" but with two reception rooms, four bedrooms and two bathrooms as well as garages and carports, they make comfortable family homes.

Above and below: Here is Aldbury in March 1923 with the car parked by the historic elm tree. Fifty years later there was an epidemic of Dutch Elm disease in the area and many fine trees were lost. This tree was injected against the disease but sadly the next year it was found to be virtually hollow and it was decided that the old tree, known as 'Bunyan's Elm', should be felled. There was a saying in the village that 'when the old tree dies there will be no more children born in Aldbury'. The elm was replaced by a young oak tree which happily is still flourishing, as is the population of Aldbury.

Above and below: For some years there had been discussion about the future of Pond Close, the open space beyond the church. Tring Council proposed that on one corner they should build a small estate of sheltered accommodation for the older people of the town. They were granted planning approval early in 1974. These homes were very popular with the tenants and when, many years later, they were threatened with demolition as repairs were needed, there were a large number of protests. The Borough Council had a change of heart and the repairs were completed. The building, though rather plain, still provides comfortable, convenient homes for local people.

Above and below: The work on the bypass was started on 7 August 1973. The constructors, Mears Construction, found they did not get as much local opposition as they had expected although the route went through Tring Park. Most people accepted that the bypass was essential for Tring and the park could still be enjoyed with very little disruption. The first photograph shows a drainage lake being dug out and the second a bridge being built near West Leith in Duckmore Lane.

Above and below: This photograph shows the footbridge reached from Park Street under construction. The bypass was opened quietly, without ceremony, on Thursday 17 July 1975. The finish was three months behind schedule but the contractor's problems included cut-backs at British Steel, three-day weeks, coal strikes, electricity rationing and later the Israeli-Arab war, which affected oil supplies. There was also a strike in the cement industry. The Tring bypass now links up with the Aston Clinton bypass at the top of Tring Hill.

Above and left: At the beginning of 1975 there was a serious fire at Rodwell's factory in Akeman Street. Firemen fought all night to control it, with six fire engines in all, from Tring, Berkhamsted, Aylesbury and Hemel Hempstead. They used a safety curtain of water to prevent the fire from spreading to the nearby museum. The fire started early in the evening while the firm was holding its annual dinner at the Crows Nest, Tring Hill. Mr F. W. Rodwell and his staff managed to save the lorries and a forklift truck and they guarded the premises during and after the blaze. Fortunately the most damage was in the storage department, including a large amount of sugar, but it was possible to carry on the business as usual as the bottling department was unaffected. The cause of the blaze was not known.

Above left and right: On Saturday 6 July 1974 there was an exhibition at Long Barn, just outside Tring, the home of popular Tring doctor Christopher Cole, now retired. In his spare time Dr Cole made doll's houses and these pictures show his scaled-down reproduction of John Bly's antique shop in the High Street. Also in the exhibition were paintings and sculptures by his artist daughter, Tessa.

Right: The photograph of John Bly's shop shows how accurately Dr Cole made his copy. When Dr Cole retired he went to Wensleydale in Yorkshire where he had bought an old watermill. He planned to restore the mill and add workshops to carry on with his hobby/ business of making doll's houses. Dr Cole was born in Tring and his great-grandfather was John Brown, who in Victorian times had started the company that later became Brown and Merry, local estate agents and auctioneers.

Above and left: In the 1970s Tring Camera Club would put on an exhibition of prints taken by their members and give colour slide shows at intervals during the day. On one panel in 1976 the pictures had a western theme. These three examples show Mike Bass as a 'wanted' outlaw, and five-year-old Susie Carlsson, the young daughter of Pat and Erik, on her pony 'Happy Face'. When published in a local paper the caption described her as 'looking for a sunset to ride off into'.

John Bly, well known as an expert in the antique world and for TV programmes like *Heirloom, Going for a Song* and *The Antiques Roadshow*; here he is posing for one of the cowboy pictures with his young sons, Julian and James.

In the 1976 Tring Festival sixteen-year-old schoolgirl Penny Ward of Miswell Lane was elected Miss Tring. The previous year's Miss Tring, Sharon Evans, handed over the title sash to Penny. In the procession she travelled in a car that was raffled for charity by Tring Lions. The local paper said, 'The happiest sight of the festival was the ten year old girl who jumped for joy when she won a car in the raffle run by Tring Lions'.

At the festival there were two shows by the Mohicans, a team of motorcycle stunt riders. Here one of their members is in full flight. There were many other displays and events including sporting contests, a display by Rothmans Flying Display team and an egg-throwing contest sponsored by Dean's Farm Eggs.

Right: In 1976 Tring Natural History Museum had to close after the discovery of what were described as 'unwelcome exhibits'. The museum had to be fumigated after the discovery of larvae of carpet beetles in the cases. Carpet beetles, common pests, are not fussy eaters. The will live on wool, horn, fur, feathers and dried animal remains.

Below: In early July 1977 Mary Chipperfield's camels came to Tring for the Tring Festival. They had been a feature of the Young Farmers Club show at Aylesbury two months before. The camels were ridden by Tring people and the winner of the finals was Tim Woodcock who was the chairman of the Tring and District Horse Association and a Tring Town Councillor. The festival was organised by the Tring Round Table to raise funds to buy a first-aid caravan for the St John Ambulance Brigade.

Above: Tring's Regal Cinema opened in 1936 and was very popular for some time, particularly during the Second World War, but closed in 1958. It re-opened for a while, both as a cinema and a theatre, but neither was successful. There was a suggestion that there should be a supermarket on the site but by the end of 1978 the old cinema was demolished and replaced by ten flats named Regal Court.

Left: This aerial view shows Regal Court being built, with the Church House just beyond it. Christchurch Road runs along the top with Goldfield Estate turning off it.

Tring ex-serviceman Gunner John Barber in the summer of 1979 being presented to Lord Louis Mountbatten. Gunner Barber was wounded in Holland in February 1945 and as a member of BLESMA (British Limbless ex-Servicemen's Association) he was invited to take part in the Royal Tournament at Earls Court. Lord Mountbatten was murdered by the IRA about six weeks later, on 27 August 1979.

Miss Winifred Baker took over Tring Junior School in 1932 and was headmistress for thirty-five years. She died in July 1980. Here she is with her pupils and one of her fellow teachers, Mr Hamilton.

Back row from left to right: Alan Kempster, Richard Collins, Michael Collier, Michael Cross, Stephen Bartram, Geoffrey Desborough, Barry Johnson, Malcom Wilkins, Douglas Green.

Third row from left to right: Christopher Side, Stephen Wells, Kaye Poulton, Patricia Wright, ?, Elizabeth Dell, Linda Booth, Maureen Champion, Howard Wells, Keith Delderfield.

Second row from left to right: Pamela Morrish, Angela Burrows, Annette Smith, Marion Wallace, Jean Horn, Margaret Wilson, Helen ?, Carol Chambers, Margaret Howard.

Front row from left to right: Anthony Butler, Brian Chub, Robert Powell, Ivor Yates, Anthony Butler-Lee, William Atkins, Colin Stevens, Martin Lovegrove.

One of the highlights at the Tring Donkey Derby on Sunday 15 June 1980 was the appearance of Red Rum – winner of the Grand National in 1973, 1974 and 1977 and runner up in 1975 and 1976. During the day, while in his horsebox, he was 'kidnapped' and taken to Stocks House at Aldbury, the home of Victor Lowndes of 'Playboy' fame. Red Rum's owner was not very happy at what was said to be 'a lark', but he was returned safely so the 'thief' was not prosecuted.

Red Rum at the event, being ridden by jockey Tommy Stack and led by his trainer 'Ginger' McCain. It was not until twenty-four years later that McCain had another Grand National winner, with Amberley House in April 2004.

four

1981-1990

A feature of the 1980s was the popular Donkey Derby, in aid of Tring Tornadoes Junior Sports Club. It was started in 1976 and was continued for some years. There were eight donkeys, ridden bareback by local people and each one was sponsored in a race. This meant that one donkey could be the local auctioneers 'Going Going Gone' in one race, and the local photographer's 'Develop and Print' in the next, and the Kings Arms' 'Royal Cuddle' in another. Some of the jockeys were not very experienced riders and many finished the race on foot.

Town Mayor Derek Townsend at the Donkey Derby with one of the Brooke Bond chimps, a highlight of the day. The chimps were there due to the generous sponsorship of local businesses. Derek said the chimp was loveable and very well behaved.

Aldbury has often been chosen by filmmakers who want their film set in a typical unspoilt English Village. The *Shillingbury Tales*, a TV series in the early 1980s, told the story of a village brass band and a pop musician who joins them. This picture shows Tring postman John Bowman watching as his bicycle is being 'borrowed' by actor Jack Douglas.

A building in Aldbury that was featured in the *Shillingbury Tales* was Folly Cottage, though only for the outside shots. Interiors were filmed on sets elsewhere where there was more room.

Opposite above: On 29 July 1981 Tring, along with the rest of the country, joined in the celebrations for the wedding of Prince Charles and Princess Diana. The streets were decorated with flags and the papers described Charles Street as 'an appropriate place for a Royal Wedding children's party'. There were games and a splendid tea in the afternoon, and in the evening there was a chicken and chips supper and a jazz band for the grown-ups.

Opposite below: The Tring Squash Club was started in the 1930s with a court at the Rose and Crown Hotel. When the Pendley Sports Centre was set up in Cow Lane, the squash club moved there and by 1975 they had four courts. The Pendley Sports Centre is made up of several clubs, including football, rugby, hockey and bowls, as well as squash. This team was photographed around 1982.

Back row from left to right: Dave Proudfoot, Howard Clarke, Bill Nissel, Ben Truman, Dave Watkins.

Front row from left to right: Graham Carr, Alan Jones, Malcom Newton, Robin Wilcox, Steve Gill.

Above and right: When the Tring Festival was held in 1983 it was estimated that 10,000 people packed into the town centre on a beautiful hot sunny day. One feature was the appointment of a new town crier and the man given the job, Brian Carter, was sweltering in a heavy, specially-designed costume. Tring had had town criers before and this early photograph of Tom Gaskin shows that he wore a similar costume. Brian held the post for seventeen years, retiring in 2000.

Some of the oldest part of Akeman Street in 1984 after it had been bought by property developers. It was a historic site that included Graces Maltings and there was concern that listed buildings were in danger of serious damage. Local residents signed a petition to protest when the developers constructed a garage across a pedestrian access, to an unapproved design. This picture of Clements Place shows work in progress.

Graces Mill in the 1970s. It was a malting in medieval times and was used as one until after the First World War. It continued as a corn mill for another fifty years, mainly in the care of Bob Grace. Bob was very well known in Tring as a councillor for many years and also as a local historian with a fund of knowledge about Tring, the home of his family for many generations.

Right: Another view of the old mill before the area was developed. The brown and white spaniel was Bob's constant companion and the bantams could often be seen in Akeman Street and neighbouring Clements Place.

Below: Part of the mill facing Akeman Street after work had started. Now known as Graces Maltings there are a collection of interesting homes retaining some of the original features.

The Tring Jogging Club was founded in 1981. Here are the team that ran the 1984 London Marathon. Standing left to right: Amanda Barlow, Chris Dove, Jill Fowler, Mary Payne, Len Cousens, Maureen Cousens, Jeff Hunter, Tony Smith, Brenda Barlow, Dave Manning, Carol Brennan. Seated: Jenny Elliott, Terry Elliott, Sue Monkman.

Above left and right: Tring Festival of 1984 was celebrated on a lovely sunny day. The theme that year was the circus. Here a group of clowns are part of the parade in the High Street, some of them on roller skates. The second photograph shows Tring children looking up at a very tall man.

In 1985 the 100-year-old marble drinking fountain, referred to as 'Tring's homeless Rothschild drinking fountain' had been put into storage by Tring Council. It was originally mounted on the wall of the old school in the High Street, just seen on the left. Older people remember when it was possible to obtain drinking water from it.

At first it was suggested that it should be attached to the wall of Tring churchyard. Then the Rose and Crown offered to find it a place outside their hotel but it was felt it should be on a wall. It was eventually mounted on the outside of the Memorial Garden's wall, seen as you come into Tring. However, it no longer supplies water for the passing traveller.

The year 1986 was important for Tring Park Cricket Club. They celebrated their 'sesquicentennial', 150 years since the founding of the club in 1836. David Kempster, a captain of the teams over the years, produced a booklet, giving a very informative history of the club. He also arranged a special celebration dinner at Lords Banqueting and Conference Centre and about 200 guests attended, all connected in some way with Tring Park Cricket Club. The guest speaker was the former Yorkshire, Somerset and England captain, Brian Close. A biography describes Brian as 'a fearless batsman who performed the double of 1,000 runs and 100 wickets in his first season in county cricket at the age of nineteen'. Here are shown some of the players, members and guests at the dinner. Back row, from left to right: Mrs Edna Hedges, F.S. Hedges, Lionel Sims, Richard Helliwell, Chris Lawson, G. Wheeler, H.P. Sharp (Middlesex), Mrs Ann Kempster, N. Doody, David Kempster. Front row from left to right: Mrs J. Haynes, Brian Close, Peter Haynes.

Right and below: In 1986 the convent school of St Francis de Sales in Tring was honoured by a visit of Cardinal Hume when they celebrated the fiftieth anniversary of the founding of the school. They organised a week of events including a tennis tournament.

Cardinal Hume, who was born in Newcastle-upon-Tyne, was ordained a priest in 1950 and was created archbishop of Westminster and a cardinal in 1976. The first photograph shows him talking to Sister Theresa Elizabeth. The other photograph shows him having a meal in the convent garden. In the centre are Reverend Warren from Aldbury Parish Church and Father McGuinnes from the Corpus Christi Church in Langdon Street. The school in Aylesbury Road is no longer a Catholic school. Now known as Francis House Preparatory School it is attended by children of all denominations.

Here Derek Townsend is with actress Anita Dobson, who played Angie Watts in *Eastenders*. She officially opened the tenth Donkey Derby in 1986 and she stayed for some time chatting to local people and signing autographs.

Twice in the afternoon of Sunday, 15 June 1986 at the Donkey Derby in Pound Meadow, there was a demonstration of wire walking by Zak Carlino who, it was said in the programme, 'performed many unique, difficult and heart stopping stunts'. The wire was considerably higher than it looks here and he crossed it on foot as well as with a bicycle and pushing a wheel barrow.

Derek Townsend has had a long career in local politics, still enjoyed with the same enthusiasm. More than once he has visited Buckingham Palace. Here he and his wife Janet are leaving for a Royal Garden party.

Stocks House at Aldbury saw several changes in the 1980s. Built by Arnold Duncombe in 1773 it was considerably altered and enlarged the following century. For a large part of the nineteenth century the mistress of Stocks was Mrs Emma Katharine Bright who died in 1891 after nearly sixty years there. She had two husbands; the first, James Adam Gordon, inherited the property in 1832. The second, Richard Bright, died in 1878. In 1892 the author Mrs Mary Humphrey Ward came to live in the house and stayed until her death in 1920. In 1944 the house became a girls' school known as Brondesbury at Stocks. It closed in 1972 and became Victor Lownes' Playboy bunny and croupier training centre. He paid £100,000 for it. In 1988 Stocks was bought by four partners for £1.6 million, and became Stocks Hotel and Country Club, chaired by hotel tycoon Mr Peter Eden. One of his partners was England cricketer Phil Edmonds.

Above and below: Early in 1989 Princess Ann, who is president of the Save the Children Fund, expressed a wish to visit the Tring shop, which was doing very well, run by Don and Patience Cartwright and their helpers. The takings then were about £40,000 a year. The Princess came in the Easter holidays so the children were able to come out to see her. In the first photograph she is being greeted by the director of the Save the Children Fund with the town mayor Cllr Tim Amsden next to him. In the other picture the young children are offering Princess Anne flowers to add to the bouquet presented to her earlier by fourteen-year-old Rosie Smith.

Right: A hundred years ago, Miss Gwendoline Knight was born in Tring on 11 April 1889. Her father, well-known local businessman Edward Craddock Knight, was killed in an accident just over a year later. His horse bolted, the trap hit the low wall of the bridge over the canal near Tring Station and he was hurled over, hitting the towpath below. Mrs Knight, who was with her husband, survived by landing in the water and she lived until 1945.

Gwen lived with her mother and as a girl was a keen member of the TYWCA's gymnast team, giving displays to raise money during the First World War. She was also a Sunday School teacher for many years. In later years Gwen was a founder member of the Fuchsia Club and belonged to many other societies.

She lived in the same house in Akeman Street for most of her life until October 1988 when she moved to the Jabula Nursing Home in Grove Gardens.

Here Gwen is with Tring Town Mayor Cllr Tim Amsden cutting her enormous birthday cake. In her left hand is the telegram she received from the Queen.

Below: Gwen in the centre of the front row with the gymnast team.

Above and below: In October 1989 work started on rebuilding the road surface of Tring High Street, which was in very poor condition. It was planned to use brick block paving and to have Victorian-style wall-mounted street lamps. The work caused chaos for several weeks but the road was finished in good time for Christmas. The opening ceremony was performed by Tring town mayor Cllr Derek Townsend and County Councillor Trevor Marwood who cut the tape.

For many years Tring had its own purpose-built post office. The first photograph was taken in the 1880s showing the new building. The second shows it in about 1910. In November 1989 it was closed down and a sub-post office was opened in a wine shop in the Lower High Street, next to the NatWest bank. Some people were critical; there was a protest from Alcoholics Anonymous saying the choice of venue was quite inappropriate. The off-licence department was later discontinued and the family-run post office still provides a good service for the people of Tring.

Above and below: The tree beside St Martha's Church survived the gales of 1987 but it came down when some more severe gales hit Tring in January 1990. Fortunately the church was unharmed, though there was some damage in other parts of the town.

The Tring Memorial Gardens were opened in 1953. By 1990 they had become overgrown, and described as 'dark and forbidding'. Work was done to improve the area with cash supplied by the town and borough councils and Charles Church Developers of Beaconsfield. Here the revamped Memorial Gardens are being officially opened by Tring Mayor Cllr Derek Townsend and Hemel Hempstead Mayor Cllr Kenneth Coleman. More than forty-five representatives of local groups attended the reopening.

In 1990 the news was dominated by the threat to Tring Park. Tim Amsden, of the Tring Local History Society, described Tring Park as 'a very ancient and special piece of our local countryside'. For centuries it belonged to the Crown and had a succession of tenants. In 1679 King Charles II granted the Manor of Tring to his groom of the bedchamber, Henry Guy, who had the Mansion built in 1682 to a design by Sir Christopher Wren. There were other owners and tenants of the estate and in 1872 it was sold by auction to Lionel de Rothschild, a wealthy banker. His son Nathaniel, the first Lord Rothschild, lived in the Mansion and took care that the park was carefully tended. As well as deer that had roamed there for years, his son Walter added more exotic animals like emus, cassowaries and wallabies.

Above and below: The annual Tring Show, the largest one-day show in the country, was held in Tring Park each year while the Rothschilds were in the Mansion and it attracted hundreds of exhibitors and thousands of spectators. Here are some smartly-dressed visitors looking round the stalls.

A more recent picture at Tring Show, taken in the 1930s, shows the beautiful mature trees that grow in the area.

In 1988 Whitbread plc bought the park for a reputed £1 million and horrified local people by trying to get planning permission to build a hotel and an eighteen-hole golf course. In July 1990 this was altered to a conference and leisure centre. In August SWAG was launched, standing for 'Stop Whitbread Abusing Green Belt' and vigorous efforts were made to safeguard the park's future.

More plans were submitted, then withdrawn, then more submitted but all were turned down. Eventually, in August 1994 Dacorum Borough Council purchased the park from Whitbread and leased it to the Woodland Trust on a long 399-year lease.

five
1991-2000

The square in front of Tring Parish Church housed the old market house, which was demolished in 1900. It left a clear view of the church but was used as a car park until 1991 when local people decided it was time to turn what had become an eyesore into an interesting focal point for the town. The square was described as 'an unfortunate mish-mash of cars, bus shelter, bollards and insensitive landscaping'.

The redeveloped church square was officially opened in January 1992 by the Bishop of Hertford, the Rt Reverend Robin Smith. In the centre is the zebra's head pavement maze designed by local architects Graham Hoad and Derek Rogers, inspired by the zebras owned by Walter, the 2nd Lord Rothschild, who trained them to pull a carriage. The plan to redevelop the square was originally the dream of Cllr Tim Amsden in 1983. A keen historian, Tim, with other members of the Tring Local History Society, is now working hard to establish a Local History Museum in Tring.

The early 1990s still saw the continuing battle to save Tring Park. Whitbread put forward new proposals, none of which pleased local people. In December 1993 it was announced that the Secretary of State for the Environment had decided that Whitbread could build four houses on a corner of the parkland and then sell the remainder of the land to Dacorum Borough Council to be leased to the Woodland Trust. This was reported as 'a great Christmas gift for Tring'. The five-year battle seemed to have been won. There was an anxious moment when the planning inspector said the building of four houses in the Green Belt was inappropriate, but in the circumstances he allowed it to ensure that the deal with Whitbread went through. The park still provides an unspoilt open space for dog walkers and ramblers, within easy walking distance of the town.

In 1991 Tring Council made a deal with the trustees of the cattle market to give them the New Mill allotments, with planning permission for houses, in exchange for the market. When the cattle market later ceased trading the council adapted the site for the Friday Market, the Farmers Market and visiting Continental Markets.

In 1992 the Royal Mail gave the redeveloped Church Square a special pillar box. It is a replica of a Victorian Penfold box that first appeared in Cheltenham in the mid-nineteenth century. The Royal Mail only gives these boxes where it feels they will add to a special heritage feature and Tring was the first one in Hertfordshire to get one. 'Christening' the box with champagne is Mike Sherring-Lucas, one of the organisers of the Victorian Fiesta. On the left is Geoffrey Dicker, Tring postman, being a Victorian postman for the day. On the right is John Savage, a Post Office official, now very much involved with the Wendover Arm Trust, restoring our local canal. The other postman is Ross Hussey.

Four well-known Tring people were in the town to publicise the first Victorian Fiesta, which took place on 26 November 1993. Around forty-five shops stayed open in the evening with many of the owners and visitors in Victorian dress. There were numerous street activities including two carousels, bell ringers, morris dancers, shire horses and a hot chestnut stall. With Queen Victoria (alias Carol Lawrence) are Mike Sherring-Lucas, Don Cartwright and Stan Mills.

Hildene, the house in Aylesbury Road built by the Rothschild estate in around 1908 for Dr Karl Jordan, Walter Rothschild's entomologist. Dr Jordan devoted his life to Tring Museum and lived into his nineties. He had two daughters, Ada and Hilda. Hilda, a keen photographer, was president of the Tring Camera Club for many years and she donated the silver cup for the best natural history photograph.

The house was later part of the Convent School premises and was demolished to be replaced by St Josephs, sheltered accommodation for the elderly, which opened in 1993. In April 1994 St Josephs was officially opened by Derek Townsend, Chairman of Age Concern in Dacorum, who unveiled a plaque.

Left and below: Early in 1994 the 240-year-old Parsonage Place barn, thought to be the oldest in Tring, was severely damaged by fire. The barn was part of the High Street business of G. Grace and Son and Gilbert Grace managed to save a customer's classic car but his own 1968 V8 Daimler was destroyed by the fire. This was just the beginning of Gilbert's problems as the barn is a historic listed building and it appeared that there were strict rules for its restoration. A seventeen-year-old boy appeared at Hemel Hempstead Magistrates Court charged with starting the fire, which was said to have caused £100,000 worth of damage.

Right and below: After the Woodland Trust secured the lease of the park the council took on the upkeep of the obelisk, known locally as 'Nell Gwynn's Monument', and the remaining portion of the summerhouse. Both are Grade II listed buildings and thought to be the work of James Gibbs (1682-1754). They are distinctive landmarks on the way through Tring Park to Wigginton. Here is the obelisk in 1994 and the summerhouse in 1995, while restoration work was underway.

The Tring Choral Society had an important event in April 1994. It was 100 years since the newly formed Choral Society performed their first concert on Wednesday 4 April 1894 in the Victoria Hall. Seven years before the centenary the Society found a programme from this concert, entitled 'Conversazione'. The organisers of the 1994 concert went to a lot of trouble to duplicate the earlier programme, eventually tracing the words and music of each item.

The concert, held in the same hall on Saturday 9 April, attracted a full house, many of the audience dressed in Victorian costume, as were the performers. Conductor and pianist Colin Stevens is in the centre. To his right is singer Rosalie Sadler, who sang two of the main items. On the left is Richard Grylls who also played the piano. Other solo singers were Peter Jones, David Hayes, Robert Davies and Sally Dussek. John Shorter, an English teacher at Tring School, talked about Britain and Tring in Victorian times.

Above and below: On a lovely July day in 1994 thousands of people flocked to the picturesque Bulbourne Lockgate workshop to see how the canal is run and looked after. It was only the second time the Victorian canalside buildings had been open to the public. Visitors could go on boat trips, see how lock gates are made and see exhibitions of boats and crafts. It was a wonderful day out for children who even had a bouncy castle to play on.

In 1995 Tring celebrated the fiftieth anniversary of VE day, the day of victory in Europe. A commemorative service was held in Tring Parish Church in the morning. In the afternoon the High Street was closed and we took a picnic there and joined hundreds of people for a street party. Chairs and tables were put out along the road, just as they had been fifty years before in many towns. After dark the day was rounded off with a beacon fire. During the afternoon a genuine Jeep was driven round the town with the 'GIs' giving lifts to the children.

Children in Dundale JMI School Nativity play, Christmas 1995. Back row from left to right: Simon Bromley, Bethany Jones, Catherine Langthorne, Amy Chambers, Victoria Wakley (above Amy), the Angel Gabriel, Katherine Steers, Lindsey Dakin, Katherine Armstrong, Harriet Goujan, Rachel Rance, Richard McKenna, Rachel Eggleton.

Front row from left to right: Elizabeth Browne, Adam Platt, Benjamin Alcock (in front of Adam), Nicolas Mann, Sophie Wright (Mary), Adam Cartwright-Howell (Joseph), James Worrell, Lee Greenwood, Daniel Kempster (far right with crown).

In 1996 there was a great deal of controversy about Sainsburys' application to build a superstore on the then disused Tring Cattle Market. Although some people preferred the more central location to that put forward by Tesco, many thought it was too close to nearby housing, too restricted for parking, and they were also worried that it would mean the demolition of the fire station. There was also fear that the old sheep pens, of historical interest, would be lost. In the end Tesco were allowed to build in the London Road. Here is the old market showing the old office building, soon hopefully to be restored as a museum by the Tring and District Local History and Museum Society.

In 1997 Tring-born Len Cousens was training to run his seventeenth London Marathon. He would by then be one of only thirty athletes to have competed in every London Marathon since its inauguration in 1981. By 1997 Len had run a total of thirty-five marathons including New York, Paris, Berlin and Barbados.

His wife Maureen was also a competent runner, competing in marathons and other events, and his son Lee joined him to run his sixth London Marathon that year.

Here is Len in training for a triathlon when the event combined swimming, cycling and running.

The bothy when it was being used by William J. Cox Ltd. This was the site chosen by Tesco for their new store in Tring.

In the mid-1990s, when Tesco applied to build a new superstore on the outskirts of Tring on the redundant site of William J. Cox plastic factory, there were mixed reactions. Many people who already shopped at stores in Berkhamsted or Aylesbury welcomed the idea. Others who felt it would finish off the smaller businesses in the town were very much opposed to it. The papers were full of 'for and against' letters stating people's views and at council meetings tempers flared on more than one occasion.

On Monday 27 April 1998 the new Tesco store was officially opened. Pupils from the St Francis de Sales School had composed a marketing jingle and they were invited to sing it at the opening ceremony. There was also music from The Syndicate New Orleans Five Jazz Band.

Cutting the ribbon to declare the store open was performed by Carol and Alistair Anderson who had fought a long campaign for the store throughout the three-year planning battle. They were treated as VIPs for the day and arrived in a Rolls Royce.

In April 1983 Cllr Bob Grace announced his retirement from the council after thirty-four years. He always stood as an independent and could be relied upon to support policies that he felt were best for Tring. He was best known as a local historian and he and his brother Tom used to give lectures with lantern slides in an old projector first used by their father, Frank Grace. He used a plate camera and made glass slides of views of Tring. In May 1997 Bob celebrated the 100th birthday of the old projector with a special 'party' and a lantern lecture enjoyed by local people.

In 1997 Crest Homes of Hemel Hempstead won their appeal for permission to build six houses on the site of the big house, Beech Grove, in Station Road. As can be seen here, in January that year Beech Grove was a fine old house. It had been the headquarters of the British Trust for Ornithology for some time. When built, the new road was called The Beeches. In Station Road two other magnificent homes had been demolished. 'Hawkwell' had become Hawkwell Drive and 'Hazely' in now Hazley Road.

Above left and right: On Sunday July 19 1998 a column of 'retired' buses came through Tring. Now privately owned and driven by enthusiasts they were a nostalgic sight going through the town. When Tring had its own bus garage and many people did not own cars the 301 double decker buses were a familiar sight. Many people went, as they still do, on the 387 to Tring Station to catch a train to London.

Buses and their drivers in Tring in the 1930s. Goldfield houses are just behind them and Miswell Lane can be seen in the distance.

Above and below: The old church tower at Long Marston dated back to about the fifteenth century, a remnant of the twelfth-century Chapel of All Saints that was there. In 1883 the main body of the chapel was pulled down, leaving the tower which, by the end of the twentieth century, was rapidly deteriorating and in a dangerous condition. A new Church of All Saints was built in 1883 just across the road from the vicarage built in 1873.

Right: In early 1999 a group known as the Tower Conservation Group was formed to try to raise funds to renovate the tower, which in 1966 was Grade II listed as an ancient monument. John Noakes, living in the nearby sixteenth-century Old Church Cottage, worked untiringly on the project, as did Oliver and Ernestine Mathews, living in the farmhouse by the tower. Oliver and Ernestine organised 'Tea at the Tower' each year and a walk round the beautiful local countryside. The old tower was saved, thanks to the Conservation Group.

Below: Tring School joined the Save the Children Fund Shop to raise money for the Tring Millennium Group Water Project. Pupils organised two days of 'Big Breakfasts', a bacon roll and a mug of hot drinking chocolate. This was obviously popular with visitors as they raised over £876. Here Jenny Brennan-Isles is handing over a cheque to Don Cartwright, chairman and tireless worker for the Tring Save the Children. The money went towards building wells in the drought-stricken Zambezi Valley in Zimbabwe.

Above and below: The original Corpus Christi Church in Langdon Street was built in 1912. It was attended regularly over the years by Tring's Catholic population but towards the end of the century it was found to be in need of restoration and an extension was suggested. Work began in September 1998 and on 27 October 1999 Father Potter was given the keys of the completed church. The first Mass of Thanksgiving was held in the church on 11 November.

In 2000 Rodwells, the soft drinks firm, moved their headquarters from Akeman Street in Tring to Berkhamsted. Their interesting old brewery was adapted to make comfortable homes described by the estate agents as providing 'a 21st century lifestyle in a 19th century setting'. They were called 'Brown's Maltings', named after John Brown, a maltster, brewer and auctioneer who built the malthouse in 1876. The area is also called 'Rodwells Yard'.

Tring Sports Clubs have had numerous successes over the years but the 1999/2000 season was a spectacular one for Tring Athletic Football Club. They won the South Midlands Senior Division Cup, the Herts. Senior Centenary Trophy, the Herts Charity Shield and Cherry Red Books Trophy. The successful team are, in the back row from left to right: Neil Austin, Matt Ruscoe, Paul Lewis, Andy Humphreys, Ian Ranger, Ralph Lewis. Middle row: Steve Thomas, Richard Vincent, John Perry, Jamie McBeath, Tom Vincent, Dave Foskett, Jamie Robbins, Steve Johnson, Andy Ayres. Front row: Will Saintey, Jeb Stewart, Gary Langdale, Mark Boniface, Mick Eldridge, Danny Robbins, Grant Mosley.

Other local titles published by The History Press

Tring 1900-1950
JILL FOWLER

Illustrated with over 200 pictures, many previously unpublished, this outstanding volume offers views of Tring during a period of enormous change, from its origins as an agricultural town to the introduction of motor vehicles and the effects of two world wars. The book includes municipal buildings, pubs and local businesses, images of weddings, celebrations and public events and creates a wonderful representation of community life in this part of Hertfordshire.

9780752426853

River Thame: History & Guide
TONY CHAPLIN

The River Thame is a relatively small river running from the foothills of the Chilterns, through Buckinghamshire and Oxfordshire, on to its confluence with the Thames at Dorchester. It flows gently through a broad, flat valley, and is one of the few areas in the country where rare black poplars grow naturally and where red kites, also once on the brink of extinction, grace the skies once again. This book is a beautifully illustrated and thoroughly readable guide to the river which will appeal to locals and visitors alike. It includes a full colour picture section and an enjoyable walking tour.

9780752443737

Around Tring
MIKE BASS AND JILL FOWLER

This excellent collection of over 400 old photographs of Tring was originally published as two volumes in the popular Archive Photographs Series and is now available bound as a single volume. The fascinating sequence of photographs forms an important pictorial record of Tring's streets, buildings and people as they experience the change of nearly 100 years, from the late nineteenth century to the 1970s. The result is a book that will give much nostalgic pleasure to all who know this town

9780752422114

Hertfordshire Writers
PAMELA SHIELDS

This new book by Pamela Shields explores the connections many writers have or have had with Hertfordshire. Jane Austen, Charles Dickens, Ken Follett, Frederick Forsyth, Victoria Glendinning, Graham Greene, John Le Carre, Claire Tomalin, George Orwell and Anthony Trollope are all included. Charles Lamb called the county, 'Hearty, homely, loving Hertfordshire' and judging by the number of literary giants who choose, or once chose, to call it home he was not alone in his sentiment. Falling more into the populist history as opposed to literature genre this book is intended as a general introduction for readers who know very little about the authors.

9780752443720

If you are interested in purchasing other books published by The History Press, or in case you have difficulty finding any of our books in your local bookshop, you can also place orders directly through our website

www.thehistorypress.co.uk